A Wisley Handbook

D0012546

Foliage Plants

URSULA BUCHAN

Cassell

The Royal Horticultural Society

THE ROYAL HORTICULTURAL SOCIETY

Cassell Educational Limited
Villiers House,
41/47 Strand,
London WC2N 5JE
for the Royal Horticultural Society

First published 1988
Second edition 1993

British Library Cataloguing in Publication Data
A catalogue record for this book is available from the British Library

ISBN 0–304–32057–9

Photographs: pp. 7, 8, 20, 21, 27, 29 (top), 32, 34 (top), 36, 47, 49, 54 (left) and 59
by Valerie Finnis; others by Photos Horticultural

Phototypesetting by RGM Typesetting, Southport
Printed in Hong Kong by Wing King Tong Co. Ltd

Front cover: Colourful foliage with, from top to bottom, *Cotinus coggygria* 'Royal Purple', rue
(*Ruta graveolens* 'Jackman's Blue') and box (*Buxus sempervirens*).
p. 1: Contrasting leaf shapes in shades of green with dogwood (*Cornus*), the grass *Miscanthus
sinensis* 'Variegata', feverfew (*Chrysanthemum parthenium*) and rue (*Ruta graveolens*).
Back cover: Golden ivy, purple cotinus and green bergenia make an attractive foliage display
in a mixed border, with irises adding a touch of extra colour.
   Photographs by Eric Crichton Photos

Contents

Introduction

Everyone knows that the word "foliage" is the collective name for the leaves of a plant or tree, but many are less certain about what is meant by "foliage plant". This is hardly surprising, considering there *is* no precise definition. Many plants have interesting, unusual or beautiful leaves, but they also flower, of course. The hosta, for example, is usually referred to as a foliage plant, yet it has pretty and quite conspicuous flowers. *Fatsia japonica* is another plant with striking flowers which one would nevertheless label a foliage plant. The most useful definition of the words "foliage plant" which I can think to offer you – a plant grown at least as much, and usually more, for its leaves as for its flowers. Fortunately, although it is necessary for me to be logical about what I include in this book, the gardener seeking to plant up his or her garden does not need to know exactly where to draw the line.

Even a moment's reflection on the subject makes one realize how many and various are foliage plants and how much they can enhance the beauty of gardens. For one thing, evergreens and evergreys (as silver-leaved sub-shrubs like artemisias are sometimes called) give colour to an otherwise brown and twiggy garden scene in winter and provide a useful solidity in summer. Deciduous foliage plants have a far longer season of interest than even such seemingly perpetual flowerers as the potentillas and there is, in many cases, the added bonus of a change of leaf colour in autumn.

Densely packed leaves, whether deciduous or evergreen, are important, and sometimes vital, as a background. Foliage is the perfect foil to colourful flowers, yet it can create its own substantial visual impact as well. Even shrubs which we do not consider primarily as foliage plants have flowers too small to be seen from a distance, so that it is their leaves which supply the initial impression. By providing an apt contrast, bold leaves serve to emphasize the airiness of many flowers.

Such is the range of plants which we can honestly call foliage plants, and such the range of uses they can be put to, that I have resolved to limit myself, arbitrarily but understandably, to hardy,

The striking blue-grey leaves of *Hosta tokudama*, which grows to about 1½ ft (45 cm) high and wide (see p.12)

or almost hardy, plants and to those which you have at least a sporting chance of finding in a local nursery or garden centre. I have arranged them in what I consider the most useful way, namely by leaf colour. However, I do appreciate that the distinctions are sometimes a little blurred, as in the case of *Acaena* 'Blue Haze', which, in the preparation of this book, has see-sawed between the grey and the blue chapters! In each chapter the plants are listed alphabetically by their botanical names, in groups, beginning with evergreen trees and ending with perennials, biennials and annuals. That seems to me the most logical way of proceeding if this book is to be any help at all in the vexed and highly complicated area of garden design. So important do I consider this subject that the first chapter is specifically concerned with the uses of foliage plants and with how felicitous plant groupings may be achieved with them. I stress the words "plant groupings" because I think that whole borders composed, artificially and self-consciously, only of foliage plants are a mistake; without the contrast of flower shape and colour, the garden changes too subtly and slowly for me, at least, fully to appreciate it.

I have described plants which I consider to be particularly good foliage plants. After all, of those on sale, some are decidedly better than others. As the choice is a personal one, it is possible that some readers' favourites may have been omitted, for which I am sorry.

I have not given details of cultivation, since the requirements of foliage plants are just like those of other plants. However, it is worth mentioning that some foliage shrubs and trees may be encouraged to produce leaves twice as big as usual, by pruning them in a particular way and then feeding them with well-rotted manure or compost. The purple-leaved hazel, *Corylus maxima* 'Purpurea', the coloured-leaved forms of elder, *Sambucus*, the purple smoke bush, *Cotinus coggygria* 'Royal Purple', *Eucalyptus gunnii* and the variegated varieties of *Cornus alba* all respond well if their stems are cut back to within 1 ft (30 cm) of the ground in March. This stooling, as it is called, also ensures that the shrubs do not produce flowers or fruits which would detract from the foliage. When carried out on eucalyptus, the plant retains its more attractive, bluer, juvenile foliage. Poplars and catalpas can also be pollarded, by cutting back the tree trunk to within a few feet of the ground. This will lead to the formation of a crown of young branches to give a good foliage effect.

The feathery yellow leaves of *Robinia pseudoacacia* 'Frisia' give a splash of colour above hostas, brunneras, variegated weigela, pulmonaria and other plants

Uses and Associations of Foliage Plants

It is all very well collecting together a disparate assortment of attractive plants which you would like to see growing in your garden but, if there is no thought as to their placing and particularly their interrelationṣhip, the result will be a formless muddle, sometimes accidentally effective, it is true, but always haphazard and chancy. Those plants which we grow as much, if not more, for their foliage as for their flowers can play many important roles – in unifying plant groupings; defining boundaries; acting as long-lasting recurring themes, focal points and foils; and providing contrasts and harmonies of leaf colour or leaf shape. It is even possible for them to combine more than one of these functions.

Evergreen foliage plants provide an unchanging (or subtly changing, in the case of some conifers) unifying theme in the garden all year. While the hectic flow of colour is supplied by flowers, the evergreens remain a constant, if understated, device for preserving the scheme from the threat of garishness. You only have to think of grass to realize how successful a massed foliage plant can be for setting off bright displays of flowers. Evergreen hedges made of yew and Lawson cypress act as a solid background to define more sharply what is growing in front, as well as to provide shelter. Evergreen climbers like *Clematis armandii* give year-found contrast of colour against a brick or stone wall.

Plants with bold ascending leaves, such as yucca, phormium, iris, sisyrinchium and ornamental grasses, make excellent focal points or accent plants for the ends of borders or beside entrances. The effect is usually heightened, rather than undermined, when the vertical flower stems emerge.

Above: A successful example of foliage associations, with *Rheum palmatum rubrum* providing the emphasis at The Dower House, Boughton House, Kettering
Below: *Ruta graveolens* 'Jackman's Blue', purple sage, *Helichrysum italicum*, *Euphorbia characias* and *Senecio bicolor cineraria* give a good mixture of leaf shapes and colours

Other good focal points can be established by using plants with very bold or large leaves, like rodgersia, rheum, gunnera, acanthus, globe artichoke and fatsia, whose foliage will draw the eye. These plants should not be overworked, of course, or their impact will be diminished. How much they should be used depends on the size of the border and cannot be dogmatically computed.

One of the most important functions of foliage plants in garden schemes is to provide contrasts of shape and texture which the eye will willingly accommodate. In this respect, far more is possible than with variously coloured flowers, which easily tire the eye with jarring contrasts. Among many possible combinations of foliage one might take as examples palmate rodgersia next to pinnate ferns (p.20), or the huge leaves of *Rheum palmatum rubrum* with euphorbias and ferny-leaved dicentra (p.8). Some feathery foliage, particularly that of conifers, is close-set and therefore looks dense, whereas the leaves of ferns are widely spaced and lighter in atmosphere.

It must never be underestimated how vital is the foliage plant's contribution to colour in the garden, nor how effective even simple associations can be. However timid you may be about colour schemes, you can scarcely go wrong massing a collection of grey-leaved plants, for instance, because, even though the foliage differs, there are only subtle gradations of leaf colour. I have to say, however, that a whole border of this kind can seem a little dull on an overcast day and I prefer small groupings. The varying colours of hostas also harmonize beautifully together, making this one of the most successful foliage plants for summer (provided slugs are kept at bay).

Plants with two-colour variegations, particularly cream and green, lighten the appearance of a border and make the planting look less dense when set close to those with uniformly coloured leaves. Gold-variegated plants create a slightly warmer and more sumptuous effect than cream- or white-variegated ones. Those plants which grow in shade or semi-shade (the golden variegated hostas immediately spring to mind) are especially useful, because gold-leaved plants often lose their brightness in shade. Curiously, combinations of gold- and white-variegated plants tend to detract from rather than enhance each other. Plants with similar variegations but different leaf shapes, such as *Hosta crispula* next to *Euonymus* 'Emerald Gaiety', work well together. Of course, such agreeable harmonies lose their force if overdone.

Variegated plants with three or four colours in the leaf, for example, *Ajuga reptans* 'Multicolor' are not easy to place; in general terms, it is safest to take account of whichever is the

10

dominant colour from a distance and include them in a scheme which requires that colour.

The use of coloured-leaved trees is much more acceptable in a garden context than in the landscape but, because of sheer mass, it is wise to group a striking tree like *Robina pseudoacacia* 'Frisia' with green-leaved trees of different foliage form or texture, or to place it on its own; next to purple *Acer palmatum* forma *atropurpureum*, for example, the effect is a little crude. In the case of coloured-foliage trees, both evergreen and deciduous, restraint is sometimes necessary: a mixture of brightly coloured dwarf conifers can be restless in their variety. Cream and green variegations can be added to a scheme if the purple is too heavy, as it can be in late summer. Thus, the variegated *Cornus alba* 'Elegantissima' would lighten the effect of *Acer platanoides* 'Crimson King', for instance, or *Prunus × cistena*.

Red, purple or pink leaves are pleasantly set off by glaucous or grey foliage. Combinations such as *Festuca glauca* and purple berberis or *Cotinus coggygria* 'Royal Purple' and *Pyrus salicifolia* 'Pendula' work well. Purple sage makes a good contrast for any grey foliage plant. Green leaves will also complement grey: *Alchemilla mollis* looks well with grey carpeters and its lime-green flowers are not startling enough to be offensive. The effect can be made more complex and satisfying by contributing bronze and blue-grey in the shape of *Foeniculum vulgare purpureum* and *Acaena* 'Blue Haze'.

The unusual brown and black tints of *Sedum* 'Vera Jameson' and *Ophiopogon planiscapus nigrescens* can be grouped with the grey-blue of *Euphorbia myrsinites* or the yellow of *Carex oshimensis* 'Evergold'. The splendid yellow form of the meadowsweet, *Filipendula ulmaria* 'Aurea', can be happily planted next to the glaucous *Hosta sieboldiana* var. *elegans* or the silver and green *Pulmonaria saccharata* 'Argentea'. These would be fine companions too for *Sambucus racemosa* 'Plumosa Aurea'.

Purple and yellow are often matched because they are complementary colours, but the combination can be over-used. The first instance of it in a garden is startling and effective, the second is already a slightly irritating cliché. Most commonly seen is a mixture of purple-leaved berberis with the yellow-leaved *Philadelphus coronarius* 'Aureus', which works quite well even when the berberis turns red in autumn.

It is possible, particularly if the gradations are not too abrupt, to make successful groupings with many different colours or, more precisely, shades of colour. It is also rare for differing shades of autumn colour to jar.

Small foliage plants, like flowers, are best planted in groups or swathes, lines or curves, in fact anything but singletons or dots. Large-leaved plants like fatsia, on the other hand, can make an impact on their own. Whatever is done should be done boldly, simply and unfussily. My personal preference is for groupings which travel diagonally towards the back of the borders rather than merely edge the bed.

It is neither necessary nor desirable to devote a garden entirely to foliage plants. Flowers are valuable for contributing seasonal interest and diversity of form, as well as for attracting wildlife. The same colour considerations apply when combining foliage plants with flowers, although it is as well to remember that flowers are often fleeting and that the dominant association may still be between the leaves of the plants concerned, regardless of how showy the flowers are.

EXAMPLES OF PLANT ASSOCIATIONS

Almost any plant permutation will work within each group below. Some suggested combinations are indicated by the numbers in brackets – i.e. all those with (1) would go together.

For a sunny border

Actinidia kolomikta (on wall) (1)
Artemisia absinthium 'Lambrook Silver' (1)
Ballota pseudodictamnus (1)
Fuchsia magellanica 'Versicolor' (1)
Helictotrichon sempervirens (1)
Ruta graveolens 'Jackman's Blue' (2)
Salvia officinalis 'Purpurascens' (1/2) and 'Tricolor' (2)
Alchemilla mollis (2)
Stachys byzantina 'Silver Carpet' (2)
Acaena 'Blue Haze' (2)

For damp shade

Hosta tokudama (1)
Ajuga reptans 'Atropurpurea' (1) and 'Multicolor' (1)
Bergenia purpurascens (1)
Euphorbia amygdaloides 'Rubra' (2)
Juniperus squamata 'Chinese Silver' (2) (if shade not too dense)
Hosta ventricosa 'Aureomarginata' (2)
Hedera colchica 'Dentata Variegata' (2)

Athyrium niponicum var. *pictum* (1)
Pulmonaria saccharata 'Argentea' (2)
Tellima grandiflora rubra (2)

For the waterside

Gunnera manicata (1)
Filipendula ulmaria 'Aurea' (3)
Iris pseudacorus 'Variegata' (1/2/3)
Lobelia 'Queen Victoria' (1/2)
Glyceria maxima 'Variegata' (1/2)
Milium effusum aureum (3)
Rheum palmatum rubrum (2)
Rodgersia aesculifolia (3)

Leaf textures and variations in green

Fatsia japonica
Juniperus horizontalis 'Emerald Spreader'
Acer palmatum var. *dissectum*
Vitis coignetiae (up tree or over wall)

Gold and purple in sun

Corylus maxima 'Purpurea' and *Catalpa bignonioides* 'Aurea'; *Robinia pseudoacacia* 'Frisia', *Cotinus coggygria* 'Royal Purple' and *Cornus alba* 'Spaethii'.

A SELECTION FOR AUTUMN COLOUR

Fraxinus excelsior 'Jaspidea'
Populus × *canadensis* 'Aurea'
Robinia pseudoacacia 'Frisia'
Ginkgo biloba
Liriodendron tulipifera
Acer palmatum 'Dissectum Atropurpureum'
Berberis × *ottawensis* 'Superba'
Cotinus coggygria 'Royal Purple'
Hydrangea quercifolia
Vitis coignetiae
Vitis vinifera 'Purpurea'

Green Foliage

As with flowers, one does not grow all foliage plants purely for their colour. Indeed, that is hardly more than half the reason. Closely linked to colour, and often influencing it, is leaf texture and there is the multiplicity of leaf shape to consider as well. The possible combinations of these variable factors is what makes the choice so enormous, so fascinating and, it must be said, sometimes rather daunting.

CONIFERS

All conifers are foliage plants, but some are considerably more interesting than others. The ones with most impact are those with striking forms as well as good foliage. Such a one is Brewer's weeping spruce, *Picea breweriana*. This makes a pyramidal shape, up to 20 ft (6 m) in time, with branches from which grey-green shoots hang down vertically.

The charm of *Chamaecyparis nootkatensis* 'Pendula' lies (like Brewer's spruce) in the fact that the branchlets hang down from the horizontal branches creating, in a well-grown specimen, a curtain of dark green foliage. This is a conifer which will grow to about 33 ft (10 m) or more high and is tolerant of an exposed cold position.

Juniperus horizontalis 'Emerald Spreader' is a completely prostrate juniper, with bright green foliage. It can spread up to 6 ft (2 m). Junipers have the advantage of being perfectly content in alkaline soils.

Ginkgo biloba is the maidenhair tree, the only living representative of an ancient order of plants. It is not the easiest plant to establish, but worth the effort, for it makes a beautiful, broadly columnar tree in time. It is a deciduous conifer and the unique (in a tree) fan-shaped leaves, partially divided in the middle, turn a buttery yellow in autumn. It is tolerant of chalk, but will need a warm sunny place if it is to do well. The best known tree in this country, although not the tallest, is the old specimen near the Orangery in the Royal Botanic Gardens, Kew, which was planted in 1762.

Acer palmatum var. *dissectum* should have a sheltered sunny position if it is to thrive (see p.16)

DECIDUOUS TREES

Acer palmatum var. *dissectum* is a very slow-growing maple, which makes a round-headed shrub rather than a tree. The palmate leaves are finely cut, with up to 11 lobes, which are themselves deeply divided and toothed. The leaves turn red or yellow in autumn. (See p.14.)

Fagus sylvatica 'Asplenifolia', the fern-leaved beech, makes a lovely tree in time, reaching more than 50 ft (15 m) high and with a wide canopy. The leaves are not uniform: some are long and narrow, others very deeply cut.

Liriodendron tulipifera is another tree with odd-shaped attractive leaves. They are mid-green, smooth, have four lobes and are cut almost square at the end. This is the tulip tree, but it does not produce its goblet-shaped, yellow-green and orange flowers until quite mature. The leaves turn yellow before falling. It is not a tree for a small garden, nor indeed for any garden north of the Midlands.

I have included *Sorbus thibetica* 'John Mitchell' for its leaves in spring; they are up to 6 in. (15 cm) long and wide, green above, silver underneath, and they open from the vertical, giving the tree the appearance from a distance of a flowering magnolia. This is one of the whitebeam section of rowans; it becomes quite a big tree, 33 ft (10 m), and is reasonably quick-growing.

EVERGREEN SHRUBS

Fatsia japonica is an "architectural" plant with very bold, glossy, dark green, palmate foliage, divided into 7 or 9 "fingers". This is a strong-growing evergreen and makes several stems which rise up, without many branches, to 10 ft (3 m) or more. The flowers are those of the ivy writ large – great white bobbles in November. Fatsias are best grown against a wall in cold districts; they thrive in town gardens because their leaves shrug off atmospheric pollution.

Santolina rosmarinifolia ssp. *rosmarinifolia* is the rather neglected green-leaved relation of the silver cotton lavender so popular with "grey borderers". It is worth growing among its silver-leaved brethren; the button-like yellow flowers go quite well with the vivid green, thread-like foliage, and it makes a neat 20 in. (50 cm) high bush, which can be tidied up with a pair of shears after flowering.

Because its tough leaves make it suitable for planting in city centres, *Viburnum davidii* has a local authority air about it. However, it seems hard to condemn a plant for guilt by association, so I try to look at it with a dispassionate eye. The oval leaves are

Above (left): *Yucca filamentosa* slowly forms clumps of evergreen foliage;
(right) *Aralia elata* does best in milder parts of the country
Below (left): *Vitis coignetiae* may be allowed to clamber into a tree or cover a
stump; (right): the large lobed leaves of *Hydrangea quercifolia* develop lovely
autumn tints

unusually leathery, with three distinct veins down their lengths. It makes a low, wide-spreading, dense mound and, if male and female are planted together, will provide bluey turquoise berries on red stems.

Yucca filamentosa has large, lovely, creamy white flowers in 3 ft (1 m) panicles, but it is, nevertheless, usually grown for the sword-shaped, green-glaucous, stiffly pointed leaves. It needs a warm, dry, sunny position and is a little winter-tender. It is well worth the effort of protecting, however, with a thick layer of peat round the base. (See p.17.)

DECIDUOUS SHRUBS

Everyone knows the horse chestnut, with its huge palmate leaves, but few have enough space to plant one. Fortunately, there is a shrubby version, more suitable for the average garden, called *Aesculus parviflora*. It spreads by suckers, so it makes a wide-reaching deciduous thicket. The white flowers, in panicles up to 1 ft (30 cm) long, open in July and August. The leaves colour well in the autumn.

Aralia elata, the Japanese angelica tree, not only has large handsome leaves, but is also an unusual shape. It is a deciduous suckering shrub, which can grow up to 33 ft (10 m), though usually reaches about 13 ft (4 m). It has few branches and those there are, are spiny. The leaves, which are doubly pinnate, can be more than 3 ft (1 m) long and are held on slightly pendulous branches. This is a fine "architectural" plant for the larger garden. The flowers are great frothy plumes of white in early autumn. (See p.17.)

Hydrangea quercifolia has leaves deeply scalloped like those of the American red oak, *Quercus rubra*, hence its specific name. The stems are woolly and the green leaves turn to red, orange and purple in the autumn. It never grows more than 6 ft (2 m), often much less, and makes a handsome, slightly pendulous, spreading shrub. Like all hydrangeas, it needs to be sited where its terminal buds will not be burned by early morning sun after a frosty night and it does best in a sheltered position. The flowers are borne in white panicles throughout the summer. They are set off very well by the smooth green leaves. (See p.17.)

Vitis coignetiae is a glorious plant. It is a very vigorous climber which will soon, with a little help, scramble up 65 ft (20 m). The leaves are an interesting bold shape, being often 1 ft (30 cm) across, toothed, heart-shaped at the base and with usually three lobes. They are glossy green above, with a thick brown felt beneath. As if that were not enough, the leaves, particularly those in the sun, turn

The unusual dark green foliage of *Helleborus foetidus* contrasts with the flowers

every shade of vermilion, orange and purple-crimson in autumn. (See p.17.)

PERENNIALS

No account of foliage plants could ignore *Acanthus spinosus*, considering that the leaves were the inspiration for the pattern on Corinthian columns in ancient Greece. However, the stately purple-hooded flowers gathered round the 3 ft (1 m) stems in July and August are almost equally striking. Be careful when weeding near this plant for the leaves and stems are spiny.

Alchemilla mollis is the darling of the flower arrangers. Its only possible fault is a tendency to seed too widely, for in all other respects it is perfect. The fresh green leaves are pretty, particularly when they have collected raindrops, and it is aptly named 'lady's mantle' because of the neat gathering of their serrated edges. The flowers, up to 20 in. (50 cm) high, are a froth of yellow-green in midsummer. It makes a most agreeable companion to silver and purple foliage plants. The dwarf species, *Alchemilla erythropoda*, is ideal for rock gardens.

Gunnera manicata is exotic in all its parts and particularly in its huge spine-backed leaves, which stand up like umbrellas blown inside out, and grace the edge of many a lake or running stream in large gardens. The leaves have been known, in favourable conditions (that is, wet and warm), to reach 10 ft (3 m) in diameter and most resemble those of a giant rhubarb on long prickly stems. The plant is not very hardy and the crown is best protected by its own leaves laid over it in winter. The flowers are curious rather

Left: The imposing leaves of *Gunnera manicata* make an excellent focal point
Right: The bold palmate foliage of *Rodgersia aesculifolia* is highlighted by the
delicacy of ferns

than beautiful: green cones, some 20 in. (50 cm) in length, appear in
spring and gradually turn brown as the season proceeds.

Helleborus foetidus has green bell-shaped flowers and is prized
by some for these, but I grow it for the thin "finger" leaves, divided
right to the "palm", because it is they which are evident for most of
the year. A rare native of British chalk woodlands, it is a very useful
plant for a shady place. (See p.19.)

Rodgersia aesculifolia is not easy to find in nurseries and garden
centres, but nevertheless worth seeking out if you have need of
something large for a moist, preferably peaty, soil. The leaf is
similar to that of a horse chestnut, except that it has seven leaflets;
it grows up to 10 in. (25 cm) long. The flower spikes are large and
white and appear in summer.

FERNS

Few people, even convinced foliage gardeners, think hard enough
about growing ferns, despite their being accommodating plants,
happy in rather dreary, shady, damp places. Their beauty is
subdued and they do not flower, but I love the myriad sorts of our
native lady fern, *Athyrium filix-femina*. 'Victoriae' for example, has
a criss-cross pattern on the green fronds, which are crested on their
margins. Also outstanding is *Matteuccia struthiopteris*, for its
bishop's crozier fronds in spring which unfurl into upright arching
branches, hence its name shuttlecock fern. These ferns are
happiest in woodland conditions.

Silver and Grey Foliage

Most, although not all, grey and silver foliage plants originate in hot dry places. That is why they usually have many little hairs on both sides of the leaves, to prevent them losing too much moisture. The use of these plants in garden design must therefore be guided by their need for light well-drained soil and full sun (indeed, the drier and poorer the soil, the whiter the leaves will become). One of the reasons that grey borders have become so popular is that the vast majority of grey- and silver-leaved plants require the same conditions. However, without a leavening of purple-, green- and blue-leaved foliage plants, it is easy to have too much of a good thing. After all, grey-leaved plants can look drab on cloudy days and the sun cannot be guaranteed to shine all summer.

Many of these sun-lovers are members of the daisy family and have yellow, often rather coarse, daisy flowers. The industrious

The grey border in the garden at Abbots Ripton Hall, Huntingdon

Left: Like most artemisias, *A. schmidtiana* 'Nana' has aromatic leaves
Right: *Convulvulus cneorum* is not completely hardy but may be easily
increased by cuttings

gardener removes these, not only because they are often
uninteresting and detract from the purity of the plant's greyness,
but also because the neat foliage looks tatty, even losing some of its
colour, as the plant comes up to flower. Because the greyness or
silveriness of these plants results from hairs on green leaves, the
appearance can change when rain wets them, so that what was a
grey border can look quite green. The leaves also tend to start green
in spring, until the hairs have grown. The sophisticated colourist
will take all these factors into account.

CONIFERS

There are few conifers which can honestly be said to be grey or
silver, rather than blue-grey (see p.39), but one such is *Juniperus
squamata* 'Chinese Silver'. The foliage is very silvery, with only a
hint of blue. It is a multi-stemmed shrub rather than a tree; the
branches point up and out and have pendulous tips. It grows to
about 6 ft (2 m) with a spread of 5 ft (1.5 m).

Juniperus 'Grey Owl' has silvery grey foliage and makes a semi-
prostrate shrub with a spread of 6 ft (2 m) or so. It is not a dense
shrub but has a pleasing airy appearance.

DECIDUOUS TREES

Among the deciduous trees, *Populus alba* stands out because of the effect of the white woolly undersides of the three-lobed leaves as they tremble in the wind. They turn yellow in autumn. This is a tree for the outer limits of a large garden, for it grows to 65 ft (20 m), with a spread of 6 ft (2 m). No poplar should ever be planted close to a house, owing to the wide-spreading roots which can damage foundations and drains.

Pyrus salicifolia 'Pendula' is a very commonly planted, small tree, mainly because it strikes people as a good choice of present for relations celebrating their silver wedding anniversary. The leaves are weeping-willow-like and very silvery, particularly in full sun. The flowers are white pear flowers, but do little to detract from the overall silver appearance.

EVERGREEN SHRUBS

The silver plants *par excellence* are the artemisias. *Artemisia* 'Powis Castle' has finely cut, silky foliage and grows to about 3–4 ft (1–1.2 m). It does not flower much, unlike *Artemisia absinthium* 'Lambrook Silver'. This is, strictly speaking, a herbaceous perennial, but it has a woody base so finds a place here. It gets to about 2½ ft (75 cm) tall and has fine silvery foliage not dissimilar to 'Powis Castle'. *Artemisia ludoviciana* var. *latiloba* ramps about a bit, being herbaceous and having a rather vigorous root system, but the willow-like uncut leaves, on lax stems, are very silver. It will grow up to 20 in. (50 cm). One of my favourites is the little *Artemisia schmidtiana* 'Nana': it makes small mounds of silky foliage.

Atriplex halimus is the shrubby version of the purslane; it thrives by the sea and is silvery grey in all its parts. It can reach 6 ft (2 m) in a favoured position. The leaves are oval and about 2 in. (5 cm) long. It is reasonably hardy.

Ballota pseudodictamnus is another sub-shrub for the sunny well-drained border. It has curving stems, greeny silver and felted, up to 20 in. (50 cm) in length. The leaves are green at first, but soon develop their white appearance and form rosettes at the tips. The July flowers are small, mauve and held in whorls of bracts. This is not a spectacular plant but a valuable one.

Calluna vulgaris 'Silver Queen' is a useful heather, whose mauve flowers do not clash with the silver grey foliage. Callunas are not lime-tolerant.

Convolvulus cneorum wins hearts wherever it is seen. The combination of fine silky leaves and restrained, white, suffused pink, bindweed flowers is wonderful. Unfortunately, it needs protection in harsh winters. In a sheltered spot, which it well deserves, it will grow to 3 ft (1 m) tall and as much across. (See p.22.)

Hebe pinguifolia 'Pagei' is one of the most widely planted prostrate shrubs because it is dependable, reasonably hardy for a hebe and useful as groundcover when planted generously. The trailing stems are composed of many grey leaves and star-like white flowers appear in May.

Helichrysum italicum is the curry plant, so-called because of the smell given off by the leaves when crushed. It is not as impressive as some silver shrubs, but its very white needle-like leaves, on upright stems to about 1½ ft (45 cm), do stand out among greens and greys and it looks good even in winter. It has the usual, not very interesting, yellow flowers at the ends of the shoots, which are best clipped off, as the leaves lose their whiteness when the plant is flowering. Like lamb's ears, *Stachys byzantina*, this is an indispensable plant if you have children to amuse. (See p. 8.)

Helichrysum splendidum is an even better plant. It is stunning as a low 2 ft (60 cm) hedge, if cut back in April and trimmed in July – a treatment which has the advantage of preventing it flowering and becoming straggly as it is wont to do. The silver-grey leaves are ribbed and have blunt tips. Also to its credit is a much hardier constitution than is normal with helichrysums.

Lavenders are probably grown as much for their flowers as their foliage, but nevertheless deserve a place here. My favourite, *Lavandula angustifolia* 'Hidcote', grows to about 2 ft (60 cm) and as much across and has purple flowers in short spikes above the narrow silver-grey leaves. It makes an excellent informal hedge or edging next to a path.

Lotus hirsutus is grown less often than its charms warrant. The trifoliate leaves are grey and intensely hairy and it has small, pink-tinged, white, pea flowers in clusters at the end of shoots and from the leaf joints. The seed pods are like reddish star-shaped beans. This shrub will reach up to 20 in. (50 cm) high and will only thrive in a light soil and in sun.

Similar in appearance to *Ballota* is *Marrubium cyllenum*, but much less commonly seen. It has pretty, grey-green, velvety leaves which are a subtle foil to silver plants.

Phlomis fruticosa, the Jerusalem sage, is almost too well known, yet despite its charms being a little overrated, it cannot be omitted from this list. It grows, in height and width, to about 4 ft (1.2 m) and has wedge-shaped, grey-green, wrinkled, furry leaves on young grey stems, which become woody in time. The hooded yellow flowers are borne in whorls at the top of the stems in July. Although reasonably hardy, it only thrives in a sunny well-drained place.

Santolina chamaecyparissus, the cotton lavender, is another silver-leaved sub-shrub which gives of its best if trimmed each April to encourage leaf growth and prevent the plant becoming too woody, and if the little yellow flowers are cut off in July to stop the plant becoming straggly. It then makes a mounded bush about 2 ft (60 cm) high and can be used for an informal hedge. The leaves are very short, about 1 in. (2.5 cm), but there are a great many of them so the shrub appears dense. There is a dwarf variety called *nana* (*corsica*), which is only half the height and more compact in habit.

Santolina pinnata ssp. *neapolitana* has longer, up to 3 in. (7.5 cm), thinner leaves and looks better, in my opinion, even though it is not always very silver. The pale yellow flowers are thickly borne, but have an evil smell. It is as well to cut the plant back after flowering to ensure new silvery growths for the winter. It is reasonably hardy and produces whiter foliage and sturdier growth if grown in fairly poor soil.

For a shrub which really does look white, *Senecio bicolor* spp. *cineraria* 'White Diamond' is as good as any, although it loses the intensity of whiteness a little as the leaves age. The leaf is less deeply cut than in another, also good, selection of the same species, 'Ramparts'. The only disadvantage of this plant, apart from its doubtful hardiness (it is often treated as a bedding plant), is that it can hardly be dissuaded from flowering.

Brachyglottis (*Senecio*) 'Sunshine' is a much undervalued evergreen shrub for a sunny position, presumably because it is so very easy to grow. Apart from a cutback in April, it looks after itself and does not take long to reach 4 ft (1.2 m), with a 3 ft (1 m) spread. It makes a rounded bush, so that two plants can look handsome placed on each side of a path or entrance. The oval leaves are grey-green above and grey-white below. I try to remember to cut off the stems which will carry the slightly coarse, yellow, daisy flowers in summer. It is reasonably hardy.

DECIDUOUS SHRUBS

Elaeagnus angustifolia and *Elaeagnus commutata* are useful silver foliage shrubs, despite being deciduous. The first is the more vigorous and can become a small tree in favourable conditions, whereas the second scarcely exceeds 6 ft (2 m). *Elaeagnus angustifolia* has narrower, more willow-like leaves than *E. commutata*. Both have small fragrant flowers in early summer, followed by small, silvery, oval fruits.

There is a dwarf willow called *Salix lanata* which has dense clusters of oval leaves covered in soft grey hairs, giving it a silvery green appearance. It rarely grows more than 3 ft (1 m) in height or width and is an ideal plant for a rock garden. The leaves are set off well by egg-shaped, golden yellow catkins in late spring. The woolly willow, as it is aptly named, is a rare native of Scotland, as well as northern Europe and Asia.

PERENNIALS

(*Artemisia* see p.23)

Cynara cardunculus is the cardoon. It used to be much prized as a vegetable, but the stems and young leaves require blanching and few people bother any more. However, it does make a striking impact as an ornamental in the large flower border because of its huge, jagged, arching, widespread clump of silvery grey, thistle leaves. The stems of the flowers need staking and are best removed unless you wish to use the blue thistles as dried flowers. The globe artichoke, *Cynara scolymus*, is similar though less silver, and the "globes" must be punctually harvested if the leaves are not to lose their lustre. Both will grow in heavy soils.

One of the more useful rock garden plants, because it will trail on the top of a low wall, is *Euphorbia myrsinites*. It has sessile leaves, which means they have no leaf stalks. The colour of the trailing stems is just the blue side of being strictly grey. The flowers are lime-green and typically spurge-like, but they do not make a great splash. (See p.36.)

The silver-leaved deadnettle, *Lamium maculatum* 'Beacon Silver', is a desirable, low, groundcover plant for a semi-shaded position, even if it does seed itself around somewhat. The leaves are smaller than the ordinary green deadnettle and, apart from a thin green margin, almost completely covered in silver-white. Rather attractive pink blotches appear on them in cold weather; these are actually caused by a disease and may reduce growth slightly. Most lamiums (like the true 'Chequers', for example) should be treated with great suspicion because of their invasive habit, but 'Beacon Silver' is relatively innocuous and certainly pretty. The pink flowers do not detract from its appearance. (See p.28.)

Pulmonaria saccharata 'Argentea' is a very good form of this white-blotched lungwort and the oval leaves are almost completely covered with silver. It is doubly welcome for being one of the few silver-foliage plants which positively relishes shady conditions. The blue and pink flowers are produced in March. A mulch of shredded bark compost put down in spring is necessary to ensure the required moist conditions throughout the growing season.

Edible as well as decorative, the globe artichoke may grow up to 6 ft (2 m) high

Raoulia australis is made up of tiny rosettes of oval leaves which seem to flow through a rock bed like a river of molten silver. It needs full sun, but is generally quite hardy, provided the winter is not too wet or the soil heavy. It has minute yellow flowers in April and May. The whole plant is no more than 1 in (2.5 cm) high.

The neat, succulent, grey-white rosettes of the ground-hugging rock plant, *Sedum spathulifolium* 'Cape Blanco' (often wrongly called 'Cappa Blanca'), contrast quite agreeably with the yellow flowers in June and July. This is an easy plant for a sunny spot in the rock garden or at the border's edge; it is also very easy to divide and propagate. (See p.28.)

Stachys byzantina 'Silver Carpet' is an improvement on the ordinary lamb's ears because the silver quality of the velvety leaves is not undermined by shaggy undistinguished flower spikes. It is an excellent edger for a sunny border.

The best of all silver perennials, in my opinion, is *Tanacetum haradjanii* (*T. densum* 'Amani', *Chrysanthemum haradjanii*). It is a mat-forming perennial which grows no higher than 6 in. (15 cm) and has leaves so deeply dissected that they look like silver-white

Left: *Lamium maculatum* 'Beacon Silver', a valuable silver-leaved plant for a shady spot (see p.26)
Right: *Sedum spathulifolium* 'Cape Blanco' spreads happily in any dry sunny place (see p.27)

feathers. The flowers resemble those of groundsel and should be removed if possible. It is reasonably hardy in a well-drained sunny position.

BIENNIALS

I dislike weeding around the biennial Scotch thistle, *Onopordon acanthium*, because the seedlings are so prickly, but I concede that it is a majestic plant for the back of a big border, even if the erect branching of the winged stems is a bit eccentric. It can reach 8 ft (2.5 m) high and will need staking. The flowers come out in late July; these should be deadheaded if the plant is to retain its silver-grey foliage effect and to prevent it sowing itself everywhere.

Salvia argentea is a most unusual plant, grown not for the mauve-white flowers dotted on the 3 ft (1m) tall stem in July and August, but rather for the ground-hugging rosette of large, intensely white-woolly, triangular-oval leaves. In a very well-drained sunny spot it may be perennial, but it is more often treated as biennial and seeds quite freely anyway if you can bear not to cut back the scruffy flower stems.

Above: The handsome *Salvia argentea* prefers full sun and a dry soil
Below: The silver-grey fronds of *Athyrium niponicum* var. *pictum* are most
unusual in a fern

FERNS

Athyrium niponicum var. *pictum* (*A. niponicum* 'Metallicum') is a
beautiful fern. The green fronds, 8 by 4 in. (20 by 10 cm) are overlaid
with silver-grey and contrast well with the deep red stems. It needs
a damp humus-rich spot in shade. Once seen, this plant is never
forgotten.

Bronze, Red and Purple Foliage

The words "purple-leaved" are much too commonly and loosely applied: plants with leaf colour as various as bronze, pink and deep red frequently have the same epithet *purpureum* tacked on to their names. For example, the bronze-green-leaved form of fennel is *Foeniculum vulgare purpureum*. However, conscious that I may drown if I swim against this particular tide, I have included all the leaf colours in this chapter normally to be found masquerading under the name *purpureum*.

CONIFERS

Microbiota decussata is a first-class prostrate conifer, whose ferny green foliage turns a rich bronze in winter. If planted in groups, it makes excellent groundcover.

DECIDUOUS TREES

Outststanding among deciduous trees is a Japanese maple called *Acer palmatum* forma *atropurpureum*. It has bronzy purple, palmate leaves which turn deep red in autumn. It grows to only about 13 ft (4 m), with a spread of 8 ft (2.5 m), and does best in a slightly acid soil to which humus has been added. Another good form is *Acer palmatum* 'Dissectum Atropurpureum'. This makes a low rounded bush rather than a tree; it has deep red, very finely divided leaves. (See p.61.)

Acer platanoides 'Crimson King' is a cultivar of the Norway maple with glossy, deep purple-crimson leaves, which appear almost black after midsummer. It needs to be placed where the sun will shine on it. It is impressive from a distance but oppressive close to. Like the other Norway maples, it becomes quite a large tree in time.

The coloured forms of the sycamore are suitable for gardens because, unlike the species itself, they do not become very large. *Acer pseudoplatanus* 'Brilliantissimum' slowly grows into a domed

---

'Royal Purple', a form with dark purple foliage of the smoke bush, *Cotinus coggygria* (see p.33)

Acer pseudoplatanus 'Brilliantissimum', a beautifully coloured, small tree, at The Dower House, Boughton House, Kettering

shape and has shrimp-pink new leaves which "go off" to a dirty green as the summer wears on. A lovely tree to gasp at in other people's gardens.

There are several types of purple beech, hardly distinguishable from each other. The deepest purple is probably *Fagus sylvatica* 'Riversii'. If you want a cut-leaved form, 'Rohanii' is the one to order. These can be used with the ordinary green-leaved common beech to make a "tapestry" hedge, although all will grow very tall. Beeches like any soil which is not too damp and a sunny position.

I am extremely attached to the hybrid crab apple, *Malus* 'Liset', even though the reddish purple colour of the leaves does not endure but turns to bronzy green as the season wears on. The flowers are deep crimson and the fruits dark red. It makes a round-headed small tree about 20 ft (6 m) tall.

EVERGREEN SHRUBS

Erica carnea 'Vivellii' is a mixture of colours which is just the right side of the vulgar. The foliage is bronze-red and the winter flowers deep carmine. This will not be everybody's choice, but it is an intriguing combination and the winter-flowering heaths have the great advantage of being lime-tolerant.

Phormium tenax 'Purpureum', the purple form of the New Zealand flax, is almost hardy, but needs some protection, such as straw round the base, if you are to be certain of getting it through the winter. It has emphatic sword-like leaves which point skywards and sometimes bend over near the tips. It flowers only when it is mature. There is a dwarf form called 'Bronze Baby' which gets to about 1 ft (30 cm). 'Thumbelina' is even smaller. Neither of the latter is very effective when massed; they are better as specimens in the rock garden.

Pittosporum tenuifolium 'Purpureum' is another rather tender evergreen, or rather, everpurple. The oval leaves on black stems of all pittosporums are distinctive because of their wavy margins and this form adds brown-purple colour as well. The deep purple flowers in spring are inconspicuous but smell deliciously of vanilla. It needs a sunny warm place and, even when suited, seems not to be long-lived.

Salvia officinalis 'Purpurascens' is also a rather short-lived and not especially hardy shrub; nevertheless it is worth bothering about if only because the leaves, like those of all forms of the common sage, can be used as a culinary herb. The leaves are velvety to the touch and of a soft, dusky purple colour which goes so well with grey foliage plants. The purple sage makes a low, slightly mounded bush, about 3 ft (1 m) across, and can be kept tidy by an annual prune in spring. (See p. 8.)

DECIDUOUS SHRUBS

Berberis × ottawensis 'Superba' is, to my mind, the best of the purple-leaved berberises, although the contest is close. It is a vigorous shrub reaching some 6 ft (2 m) high and across in time, with branches growing upward and arching at the top. The leaves turn a beautiful bright red in autumn before falling. The flowers are yellow and not a major asset to the plant. The berries are red.

Corylus maxima 'Purpurea' has rich purple leaves which also redden in autumn. The coarse and matt leaves of this purple form of the filbert make a good background for finer, lighter leaves. It is a shrub or tree which will attain 16 ft (5 m) in time, unless stooled every two years or so. Interestingly, the catkins and the nuts are also purple.

Cotinus coggygria 'Royal Purple' grows to 8 ft (2.5 m) each way in time and, planted in a sunny place in not too rich a soil, will have

Above: *Pieris* 'Forest Flame' is similar to *P. formosa* var. *forrestii* 'Wakehurst' but of more elegant habit
Below: *Vitis vinifera* 'Purpurea', a highly ornamental grape vine

deep purple leaves which become translucent red in autumn. The common name of the magnificent shrub (or, rather, of the species) is smoke bush, because of the misty masses of tiny purplish pink flowers which it bears in June or July. The combination of colours is very striking. (See p.30.)

Pieris formosa var. *forestii* 'Wakehurst' is for acid soils only, unfortunately, for this is an eminently desirable shrub. The foliage is brilliant scarlet when young and gradually turns to pink, then white, finally green. Pendulous panicles of white bell flowers are borne in May. It grows to about 6 by 5 ft (2 by 1.5 m). To do well, it should be planted in semi-shade and sheltered from cold winds.

Prunus × cistena is the best of the several purple-leaved cherries. The leaves are small, oval and a deep reddish purple; these contrast well with the small but numerous white flowers in March and April. The shrub makes an excellent hedge and should be pruned after flowering. If left to its own devices, it does not grow much above 6 ft (2 m).

Much loved by flower arrangers is the species rose, *Rosa glauca* (*R. rubrifolia*), which can boast grey-purple leaves on reddy purple stems. It is a vigorous shrub which will reach 10 ft (3 m), with a spread of 5 ft (1.5 m). No one grows this rose for its flowers, which are short-lived, small, single and pink, but autumn brings attractive, round, red hips. Seedlings are frequently found nearby. It should be planted in full sun if the leaves are to colour well.

Vitis vinifera 'Purpurea', a form of the common grape vine, colours differently from many purple-leaved shrubs: it starts deep red and becomes purple in autumn. It does produce grapes in hot summers and these, being purple, enhance the imposing effect, but do not taste pleasant. The grapes are also definitely not for winemaking.

PERENNIALS

Like all bugles, *Ajuga reptans* 'Rubra' is a thoroughly useful, without being stirring, plant. They make good groundcover in moist, partially shaded places, but will tolerate other conditions as well. This form has reddish purple, glossy green leaves which look their best in autumn. The contrast between leaves and deep blue flowers borne in whorls on 4 in. (10 cm) stems in summer is not unpleasing.

Bergenia purpurascens is one of the best of these useful evergreen perennials. The elliptic leaves, which turn inwards and point upwards and so are less good for groundcover than others of the genus, become bright purple-red in winter and then they are very

The curious dark leaves of *Sedum* 'Vera Jameson' mingle pleasantly with the blue-grey of *Euphorbia myrsinites*

ornamental. The magenta flowers are held on $1\frac{1}{4}$ ft (40 cm) red stems in April and May.

Euphorbia amygdaloides purpurea needs part shade and moist conditions, if it is not to get mildew, and is useless as a single specimen as several are required to make an impact. It is, never-theless, an interesting plant – worth growing if you have the conditions to please it. The leaves are dark green, suffused with purple; small lime-green flowers are carried on maroon stems in spring.

Foeniculum vulgare 'Purpureum' is at present a vogue plant, for its bluey bronze foliage, so finely cut as to be almost hair-like, is a welcome muted contrast to grey-leaved plants and is edible to boot. A close relative of dill, fennel bears the same yellowish green flowers, but on 5 ft (1.5 m) stems. It is best placed where the sun will shine through it.

Lobelia 'Queen Victoria' bears little resemblance to the half-hardy lobelia so much used in summer bedding schemes. For one thing, the flower stem grows up to about 3 ft (1 m); for another, it is a short-lived herbaceous perennial. It has vinous purple leaves and stems and scarlet flowers in August and September. It needs protecting with peat as it is not completely hardy.

Ophiopogon planiscapus 'Nigrescens' is a bizarre little plant which looks a bit like tufted grass at first sight. Actually, the colour of the leaves, which is retained all year, is intensely dark purple-brown rather than black, in the same way that so-called "black" hair is really deep brown. The very narrow strap-like leaves get to about 6 in. (15 cm) long and spread out from the tuft almost horizontally. This plant has tiny mauve flowers in August and sometimes black berries in autumn. It must have good moisture-retentive, yet well-drained, soil to thrive. It will increase slowly by its underground stolons.

Rheum palmatum rubrum is the purple-red-leaved form of the ornamental rhubarb and ornamental it is too. It has huge palmate leaves on 3 ft (1 m) stalks, which fade to green after the plant has flowered. The pinky red flowers are produced on 5 ft (1.5 m) long stems in June, followed by striking, brown, flat seed pods. It revels in a moist, humus-rich soil. (See p. 8.)

Saxifraga fortunei 'Wada' likes cool, shady, moist conditions where it will make a clump. This is a very good form, with rounded lobed leaves which are a reddish brown-purple on top and crimson-pink below. The white flowers, with their uneven-sized petals, are a good contrast when they come out in October and November.

Sedum 'Vera Jameson' is a most unusual but desirable stonecrop, for the succulent leaves are a curious purple-bronze, bordering on the brown, held on floppy fleshy stems. Flat heads of grey-pink flowers are carried on 1 ft (30 cm) stems in autumn.

Tellima grandiflora rubra is an excellent plant which will grow even in dry shade. The purple-bronze leaves persist all year. It is much better than the ordinary green species, although it has the usual tellima flower spikes of not very exciting, small, greeny yellow bells on 1½ ft (45 cm) stems from April to June.

Trifolium repens 'Purpurascens Quadrifolium' is a four- (or five- or six-) leaf clover with a difference but, one hopes, just as lucky. Its leaves are purple-brown with green margins. Clovers are not difficult to grow (this is a form of white clover, a common weed of lawns), but they appreciate a good moisture-retentive soil. If happy, it will cover the ground well to a height of 4 in. (10 cm). It is another plant to grow if you have children to amuse.

Viola labradorica is a native of Greenland and Labrador, not surprisingly, with small pansy flowers of bluey mauve in late spring. The form *riviniana purpurea* is grown more for the heart-shaped leaves which are a dark greenish purple, especially when young. It comes true from seed and spreads also by underground stems. It seeds itself into crannies in an unvexatious way, looking particularly pretty in the cracks between limestone paving.

ANNUALS

Atriplex hortensis var. *atrosanguinea* (*A. hortensis* var. *cupreata*) is deep beetroot purple and seeds itself about, so need not be renewed every year. It is plainly a relative of the weed, fat hen, for it is slightly succulent and has triangular leaves. It grows to 4 ft (1.2 m) and thrives in full sun. The leaves can be eaten like spinach.

Blue Foliage

Those plants which we loosely call "blue" are, really speaking, blue-grey. They are most usually recognized by the suffix 'Glauca', a word which, like 'Purpurea', embraces a multitude of variation — and wishful thinking. There are few "blue" foliage plants, just as there are few blue-flowering shrubs. Those that will pass muster are very valuable to the garden designer.

CONIFERS

Abies concolor 'Compacta' is, to my mind, the best dwarf silver fir. It makes a small compact shrub with a dense habit. The foliage is a strong grey-blue, particularly effective in late spring and early summer. It grows very slowly, eventually reaching 3 by $2\frac{1}{2}$ ft (1 m by 75 cm). Firs are not difficult to grow, although they are happiest in acid soils.

Cedrus libani atlantica 'Glauca' is not a tree for small gardens, although it is often to be found in them. It is a lovely, silvery blue in colour, pyramidal in habit, and with branches which sweep to the ground.

Chamaecyparis lawsoniana 'Pembury Blue' is the best known of the blue-grey Lawson cypresses. It is of a pyramidal shape and reaches 10–13 ft (3–4 m) by 5 ft (1.5 m) in ten years. It is deservedly popular.

Chamaecyparis pisifera 'Boulevard' is as striking in its way as 'Pembury Blue'. The colour of the soft foliage is intensely silver-blue, particularly in the summer. It never becomes a huge tree, more a conical large shrub. It repays being grown in good, slightly acid soil, in some shade.

There are many "blue" junipers, all much of a muchness. I think *Juniperus horizontalis* 'Wiltonii' the best; it is a most attractive, completely prostrate shrub, with thin, glaucous, "whipcord" tips to its long horizontal branches. In ten years it will have spread about 5 ft (1.5 m).

Juniperus scopulorum 'Blue Heaven' is a good cultivar to grow.

'Blue Heaven', one of several blue or silver cultivars of *Juniperus scopulorum*

The foliage is blue and so are the "berries". It is closely related to *J. scopulorum* 'Sky Rocket', but of a more intense blue and with a pyramidal rather than columnar habit, growing over 6 ft (2 m) in time. It thrives in full sun.

Juniperus squamata 'Blue Star', on the other hand, is a dwarf shrub, though with much the same colour of foliage. It is almost prostrate and associates well with heaths and heathers.

There are several kinds of blue *Picea pungens* on the market. As good as any is 'Thomsen', which has strongly silvery blue foliage and an erect habit. It reaches about 25 ft (8 m) in ten years but spreads only 10 ft (3 m).

EVERGREEN SHRUBS

Coronilla valentina ssp. *glauca* is grown as much for the blue-grey pinnate leaves as for the yellow, scented, pea flowers, which come in a flush in early summer and then intermittently throughout the rest of the year in fine weather. It should be grown as a wall shrub in all but the mildest districts and needs occasional trimming for it is naturally a rather floppy shrub.

Eucalyptus gunnii is favoured by flower arrangers for the blue, round, perfoliate (that is, round the stem) juvenile leaves. The 4 in. (10 cm) long, sickle-shaped, adult leaves are not so blue, but this tall tree can be stooled to retain the juvenile leaves. It must have a stake, as it is vulnerable to strong winds.

Hebe pimeleoides 'Quicksilver' is a small, evergreen, spreading shrub, 1¼ ft (40 cm) high, with very good silver-blue leaves on thin dark branches. Small white flowers appear in early summer. It appreciates a sunny place and light soil.

Othonna cheirifolia is not a plant you see very often, although I do not know why. It seems perfectly hardy here in the cold east Midlands, where I grow it over a low wall. It has unique, paddle-shaped, blue-grey leaves on erect young shoots and yellow daisy flowers in June. The whole plant does not get higher than 1 ft (30 cm) and it is not really suitable for massing but, nevertheless, the leaves contrast agreeably with those of other sun-loving foliage plants.

Ruta graveolens 'Jackman's Blue' is a well-known foliage plant of round bushy habit, with deep blue-grey leaves which are pinnate, up to 5 in. (12 cm) long and rounded at the ends. It is a sun-lover and likes a well-drained soil, but is hardy. It has yellow, not very pleasant-smelling, flowers in summer and it seeds itself about. To maintain a neat bush, trim over in April. The foliage has a bitter aroma and can cause a rash if touched with bare hands. (See p. 8.)

Left: Hostas are indispensable foliage plants and *H. sieboldiana* var. *elegans* is among the most eye-catching
Right: *Othonna cheirifolia*, a low-spreading evergreen shrub from North Africa

DECIDUOUS SHRUBS

Berberis temolaica is not easy to find in nurseries, but is worth growing for its glaucous leaves and purple shoots, and it will slowly grow to about 6 ft (2 m). The flowers are pale yellow, the berries red. It is a striking shrub, particularly in spring when the combination of yellow flowers and blue-grey leaves is very effective.

PERENNIALS

Acaena 'Blue Haze' is a little carpeting plant from New Zealand, with very blue-grey, divided, pinnate leaves and reddy brown burrs. It grows more strongly than other acaenas and makes an impact when planted in a small group. It reaches about 8 in. (20 cm).

Festuca glauca is the well-known blue fescue, a tussock-forming non-spreading grass about 10 in. (25 cm) high. It has thin, silvery blue, evergreen leaves but, unless massed, it can look a little forlorn.

Helictotrichon sempervirens is a larger blue grass, which makes a tussock of spiky leaves of about 3 ft (1 m). The flower heads are yellow and borne on arching stems. It requires a sunny position in a light soil.

Hosta sieboldiana var. *elegans* has large, blue-grey, oval, corrugated leaves, as much as 10 in. (25 cm) wide and 1 ft (30 cm) long, held on long erect stalks. The flowers are pale mauve and are not exceptional. There is a smaller version, *Hosta tokudama* (see p.4). These hostas do best in a humus-rich soil, in part shade.

Gold and Yellow Foliage

A great many plants have a yellow- or golden-foliage form; it is a frequent aberration in the plant world. Our gardens would be much poorer if that were not so, although there are some yellow-leaved plants which simply look ill and give no pleasure. Pretty or not, the fact that the leaves are yellow usually, though not inevitably, means a diminution in vigour because the chlorophyll in the leaf has been masked by another pigment like carotene. The yellow leaves of deciduous plants are often vulnerable to being burned up in bright sunshine, yet few plants colour well in deep shade. "Reversion" to green leaves is a problem, as it is with variegated plants. Nevertheless, despite these disadvantages in cultivation, yellow-leaved plants are a vital element in the foliage garden, often contributing colour when there is nothing else that will do so. This is particularly true of yellow conifers and I have tried to select forms of conifers, from the masses available, which retain some good colour in winter.

CONIFERS

Chamaecyparis lawsoniana 'Lane' is quite an old variety but is still worth growing, because it does not take up much room, being narrowly columnar in shape. In time it grows to 33 ft (10 m) or more, but will only be 6 ft (2 m) wide. It needs a place in full sun.

Chamaecyparis obtusa 'Nana Aurea' is a proper dwarf conifer, for it never grows to more than 2 ft (60 cm) each way and often considerably less. This makes it an ideal candidate for the rock garden or a raised bed in full sun. It becomes a mounded shrub with rounded fans of golden yellow foliage.

Cupressus macrocarpa 'Goldcrest' and 'Donard Gold' are similar; of the two, I marginally prefer 'Goldcrest', which has feathery, reasonably dense, bright yellow foliage. These plants are perfect for southern coastal gardens as they are wind-resistant but not really quite hardy. Neither exceeds 23 ft (7 m) when mature.

Most yellow yews, however garden-worthy, do not keep their colour well in winter. The exception is a form of the common yew, *Taxus baccata*, with ascending branches, called 'Semperaurea'. It

Robinia pseudoacacia 'Frisia', a graceful and distinctive small to medium-sized tree

The soft yellow foliage of *Acer shirasawanum* forma *aureum* remains effective throughout the summer

is a slow-growing shrub rather than a tree, wider than it is tall, up to about 10 ft (3 m) eventually and as much as 16 ft (5 m) wide.

There are several coloured forms of *Thuja occidentalis*, but two of my favourites are 'Sunkist', a slow-growing dwarf conifer, up to 3 ft (1 m) or so, with a pyramidal habit, which retains its bright golden colouring reasonably well; and the well-known 'Rheingold', which is golden in the summer, turning to a coppery bronze in winter. This makes a slightly taller conifer than 'Sunkist', though slowly, so it is excellent as a pyramidal accent plant in a small garden.

There are other fine conifers but many, like the handsome *Chamaecyparis pisifera* 'Plumosa Aurea', acquire a distinctly greenish look as the season wears on. Some people enjoy the change because conifers can stay too much the same all year round; the trouble is that the yellow forms can look very washed out as the colour starts to fade.

DECIDUOUS TREES

Acer pseudoplatanus 'Worleei' makes a tree rather than a shrub, but is still less vigorous than the ordinary sycamore, growing to about 33 ft (10 m) in time. The golden yellow leaves turn green as the summer wears on.

Acer shirasawanum forma *aureum* is a good, yellow-leaved, small tree which retains its colour until leaf fall. It is slow-growing and

44

therefore ideal for the smaller garden. This maple is best grown out of full sun, which would scorch the leaves, and does not thrive in a chalky soil.

Catalpa bignonioides 'Aurea' is the yellow-leaved form of the Indian bean tree. It will become a large spreading tree of 33 ft (10 m) or more unless, as is sometimes recommended, it is pollarded by cutting it right back to a short stump in winter. If this is done, it will grow as a shrub and its huge, soft yellow, heart-shaped leaves can be associated with other garden plants. Where space is ample, I think it should be allowed to be a tree. The colour of the leaves remains until leaf fall, indeed, if anything, it gets better.

Fraxinus excelsior 'Jaspidea' is a form of the common ash which has golden yellow shoots in spring and leaves turning yellow again in autumn. The bark is yellow as well, so it makes an interesting skeleton in winter. Ash trees are easy to grow, but should not be planted near buildings as they have far-searching roots and become very tall.

Gleditsia triacanthos 'Sunburst' is a revelation to those who see it for the first time. The pinnate leaves are attractive in themselves and they have the added charm of being the clearest brightest yellow. The yellowness does not remain and the flowers, unlike those of most members of the pea family, are insignificant, but I still think this small tree is worth growing, if you have room, for its spring splendour. It needs a sunny sheltered position in good soil.

Populus × *canadensis* 'Aurea' grows to 80 ft (25 m) or so, but can be stooled or pollarded, which is a good idea in small gardens. The heart-shaped glossy leaves are not so much yellow as yellow-green, but they turn properly yellow again before falling. Poplars are unfussy as to soil and thrive in damp conditions, but must be planted at least 65 ft (20 m) away from houses or drains.

Robinia pseudoacacia 'Frisia' is widely grown but I, for one, never tire of seeing it, particularly in the early autumn when the sulphur-yellow pinnate leaves turn more golden before falling. Like all acacia relatives (this goes for *Gleditsia* as well), it has brittle wood, so should be planted in a sheltered place. It grows to about 33 ft (10 m), making a broad-crowned tree. (See pp.7 and 42.)

EVERGREEN SHRUBS

I can happily do without most of the yellow-leaved heaths and heathers because they look so awful when their pink or mauve flowers are out. But there are some, notably *Calluna vulgaris* 'Beoley Gold', which have white flowers. When flowering in

August and September, this calluna gets to about 1 ft (30 cm). It requires full sun and acid peaty soil.

Choisya ternata 'Sundance' is the yellow-foliage form of the Mexican orange blossom. It is a most effective shrub in a sunny, sheltered, well-drained spot. It grows to about 3 ft (1 m) high and wide and has fragrant flowers in May. The foliage colour is good, although older leaves do go green.

Hebe armstrongii is one of those easy-to-grow, useful, dwarf, evergreen shrubs for which there is always a place in the garden. It is, like all hebes, questionably hardy in exposed positions or on heavy soils, but in full sun it lasts well enough. The foliage is hardly recognizable as that of a hebe, being of the 'whipcord' type, with tiny, overlapping, scale-like leaves which are golden-green in colour. The small white flowers in summer do not measurably improve its appearance. It grows up to about 2 ft (60 cm) eventually, with the same spread, and associates well with other foliage plants.

DECIDUOUS SHRUBS

Berberis thunbergii 'Aurea' is a desirable deciduous shrub, provided you do not mind a plant which gives up all pretence of having coloured leaves half way through the summer. It is slow-growing, eventually reaching 3 ft (1 m) or so. The habit is dense and basically upright, the stems deeply grooved and the round leaves are crowded on the branches, which are armed with sharp thorns. This is not a plant to tangle with unnecessarily. It does best in partial shade and a sheltered place, where the morning sun will not scorch the frosted shoots in early spring. It is easy enough to grow in ordinary garden soil.

Cornus mas 'Aurea' is not widely available, but is well worth seeking out. It is a form of the cornelian cherry and has clusters of small yellow flowers early in the year before the leaves open. When the oval leaves appear, they are golden yellow all summer. It is a bushy shrub which grows to about 8 ft (2.5 m); it needs a sunny place to flower well.

Philadelphus coronarius 'Aureus' is a winner in the right place but difficult to manage. In too much sun, the leaves brown and curl up; in too much shade, they are lime-green. Even if you get the balance right, I think it is unattractive when it flowers, for white and yellow do not always go well together. I believe it is best to trim it in spring to prevent flowering; it can look very striking as a clipped specimen in grass. The mock oranges are not particular about soil.

Sambucus racemosa 'Plumosa Aurea' is another plant which should be prevented from flowering, as the panicles of yellow-

The yellow leaves of *Berberis thunbergii* 'Aurea' turn pale green by late summer

white flowers do not look particularly good with the foliage. The divided, deeply incised, pointed leaves start off coppery and become yellow and, in the early summer, the young ones which are still growing contrast with those which are mature. The elder can be hacked about without hurt so, if you do not like the panicles of flowers in April and May, cut it back hard in the winter.

Spiraea japonica 'Goldflame' is a vogue plant which pleases me early in the season, but less so as the golden yellow colour becomes more dispersed and the rose-red flowers are borne in late summer. However, it will grow in some shade and is not more than 3 ft (1 m) in height when established. It is useful, hardy and uncomplaining.

PERENNIALS

Filipendula ulmaria 'Aurea' is the yellow-leaved meadowsweet and a good choice for a shady moist spot. It is usually recommended that one remove the creamy white flowers to encourage new golden leaves to grow in the autumn and to prevent the older leaves from turning green, but the flowers are so sweetly scented that it rather goes against the grain to do so. This plant grows to about 1½ ft (45 cm); the leaves are pinnate and deeply veined and held on horizontal stems.

Humulus lupulus 'Aureus', the yellow-leaved version of the hop, is a vigorous herbaceous climber and looks particularly good on the wall of a limestone or pale-bricked house. The leaves are coarsely toothed, furrowed, in three lobes and golden yellow. It can also be allowed to scramble through a loose shrub or up a tree or over a hedge. It is not as often enough grown as it deserves. It does best in a good moisture-retentive soil.

Milium effusum aureum is known as Bowles' golden grass, after E. A. Bowles, the great amateur botanist and plantsman, who popularized it. It is always a pleasure to come across this plant lighting up a shady corner in an enthusiast's garden. It makes a small clump of upright leaves, only about 1 ft (30 cm) high; even the

Filipendula ulmaria 'Aurea', a delightful form of the native meadowsweet or queen of the meadows

Bowles' golden grass is a useful golden-leaved plant for a shady situation

"flower" stems, which are also yellow, reach only about 1½ ft (40 cm) and are very delicate. It seeds about a little, quite inoffensively.

The Golden Marjoram, *Origanum vulgare* 'Aureum', is not a thrilling plant but it is a cheerful body for quite a sunny place and has the bonus of being a culinary herb. It gets no higher than 1 ft (30 cm) and is very useful as groundcover or as edging for a border.

Valeriana phu 'Aurea' loses its bright green colour in a few weeks, yet while at its best it is irresistable and afterwards it blends in pleasantly enough. Unlike the wall valerian, which can be such a nuisance, this is a well-behaved plant. It has 3 ft (1 m) stems of small white flowers in June, which may need staking, but it is for the yellow elliptical base leaves and deeply cut stem leaves that we grow it. This is a plant to consider if you have room for something which does not pay its way all year.

Above (left): The variegation of *Populus candicans* 'Aurora' develops best on long shoots; (right) *Aucuba japonica* 'Picturata' has conspicuous yellow marking on the leaves

Below (left): *Ilex × altaclerensis* 'Golden King', an outstanding variegated holly; (right) *Lonicera japonica* 'Aureoreticulata' is ideal as a climber or as groundcover

Variegated Foliage

Variegation, that is, the presence of two or more colours in a leaf, is a common occurrence in plants. There are many different combinations – cream and yellow; yellow and green; pink, green and white; even, in the case of *Hydrangea macrophylla* 'Quadricolor', yellow, cream, grey and green. The leaf of *Ajuga reptans* 'Multicolor' is a strange concoction of red, pink, cream-yellow and bronze.

In some plants, the colour other than green is on the margin, for instance, *Elaeagnus × ebbingei* 'Gilt Edge'; in others it is in the middle, as in *Elaeagnus pungens* 'Maculata'. Some leaves are splashed, some speckled, some mottled. The variations of variegation all make for great fun for the gardener, although variegated plants are not always easy to place.

Variegations arise for a number of reasons, but most often as a result of genetic mutation which has occurred in a green-leaved plant. That being so, reversion back to plain green leaves is a constant danger and, when seen, must be removed, otherwise the superior vigour of the green plant will swamp the variegated parts and spoil the look of the plant. Variegated plants are, generally speaking, not as strong-growing nor as sturdy as green plants, so they need more careful attention and placing. From the aesthetic angle, too, one must be careful not to over-use variegated plants, for a little goes a long way.

DECIDUOUS TREES

Acer platanoides 'Drummondii' is a striking variegated tree, much planted by local authorities in public parks. Unfortunately, the leaves revert all too easily and the aforementioned councils rarely get round to cutting off the offending branches. It has distinctive white margins to the pointed leaves and is less vigorous than the ordinary Norway maple, rarely attaining even 50 ft (15 m) and 33 ft (10 m) across. It is a good choice for a specimen tree.

Populus candicans 'Aurora' is also a good specimen tree and, being a poplar, it can be stooled or pollarded every year in March if you wish to make the most of the heart-shaped leaves. It is the youngest of these which are the most colourful; they are green, splashed and marbled with creamy white and pink.

EVERGREEN SHRUBS

The spotted laurels are on my list of least desirable shrubs, for the combination of yellow speckling on dark green leaves, with anaemic young growths, is awful. However, I concede that they will grow even in polluted atmospheres and in dry shade, where nothing much else will prosper, and there is one, *Aucuba japonica* 'Picturata', which is very much better than the rest. The leaves are properly splashed instead of just being spattered. The two sexes are on different bushes, but I should not bother to grow more than one, as the red berries add a discordant note. (See p.50.)

There are no more garden-worthy foliage shrubs than the evergreen elaeagnus, particularly the variegated forms; they are always striking, seeming brightest in the winter, and they are unfussy about soil or position. *Elaeagnus pungens* 'Maculata' has glossy green leaves with great splashes of butter-yellow in the middle, whereas *Elaeagnus × ebbingei* 'Gilt Edge' has the yellow along the margins. Both get to be quite large shrubs in time if you are not tempted to remove *all* the branches for flower arranging. (I do not know what flower arrangers did before these shrubs became widely available.)

There are some good forms of *Euonymus fortunei* var. *radicans*, some of which trail and some of which make humpy little shrubs. 'Emerald 'n' Gold' and 'Emerald Gaiety' are two of the latter. I grow them together and, although they have been slow to get going and have never gone beyond 1½ ft (45 cm), they do complement each other quite well. The first is green with an irregular, greeny yellow margin, the second green with a white irregular margin. The leaves take on a pinkish tinge in cold weather. They will grow in sun or part shade and in any reasonable soil.

Griselinia littoralis 'Variegata' is only reliably hardy on the coast, where frosts are uncommon, while its glossy leaves can withstand the salt spray. The variegation consists of great splashes of creamy white on the green leaves. If winters are mild, this shrub will grow to about 6 ft (2 m) and 4 ft (1.2 m) across. It is striking enough for any gardener to wish to take a chance with it in a warm spot.

There are so many variegated ivies it is hard to decide which of them merit inclusion. *Hedera colchica* 'Dentata Variegata' is certainly one of my favourites. The leaves are basically dark green, with light green and creamy yellow markings. They are very large, up to 8 in. (20 cm) long and 7 in. (18 cm) wide. This vigorous climber looks well growing over a tree stump or up a wall, even one facing north. *Hedera algeriensis* 'Gloire de Marengo' ('Variegata') is not dissimilar, except that the marginal variegation is creamy white. It is less hardy. These two ivies look good together. So do the much smaller-leaved *Hedera helix* ssp. *helix* 'Orodi Bogliasco' ('Goldheart'), which has a big splash of yellow in the centre of the triangular leaves, and 'Buttercup', which is all yellow and, therefore, not very vigorous. These ivies are self-clinging once established, which is a boon for the busy gardener or for anyone whose house walls will not take nails easily.

Ilex × *altaclerensis* 'Golden King' is a fine holly which can attain 23 ft (7 m) with a spread of 16 ft (5 m) but, like all variegated hollies, can be painfully slow to grow. The leaves are scarcely spiny, which is nice, and have golden yellow margins. It is a female, I have to say, which means large red berries in autumn. These frankly do not improve the look of it, but they are usually quite quickly eaten by the birds. (See p.50.) This holly looks effective grouped with white-variegated ones like *Ilex aquifolium* 'Silver Milkmaid' or 'Silver Queen'. The former has the white splash in the centre, whereas the latter has white margins. Both of these are male and do not produce berries.

Ligustrum ovalifolium 'Aureum', the golden privet, is closely related to the much despised common privet and itself comes in for some criticism. However, it grows less quickly, so does not have quite the same demand for trimming, and the colour is very bright and cheering. As a free-standing bush, it will get up to 6 ft (2 m) or so and, if allowed to flower, it has white panicles in July. The scent is too heavy for my taste. The leaf which is, naturally enough, oval, is yellow except for the very middle where it is green. It is semi-evergreen.

Lonicera japonica 'Aureoreticulata' has, as its name suggests, leaves netted with gold on all the veins; this characteristic gives it a most unusual look for a honeysuckle. It is a vigorous climber but needs a sunny position and, even so, may lose its leaves in harsh winters. It does flower in summer but not very significantly or generously. The flowers are yellow and scented. (See p.50.)

Pieris japonica 'Variegata' is a startling plant. It has narrower oval leaves than its wholly green counterpart and the margins are creamy yellow. The young leaves are flushed with pink. It makes a dense shrub and is a slow grower which will reach 10 ft (3 m) eventually. Unfortunately, it is a resolute lime-hater.

One of the loveliest variegated shrubs is *Rhamnus alaternus* 'Argenteovariegata'. This reasonably fast-growing evergreen has small, oval, grey-green leaves with irregular, creamy white margins. It gives of its best in full sun.

Salvia officinalis 'Icterina' and 'Tricolor' are both delightful. 'Icterina' is the golden sage and its new foliage is yellow, gold and

Left: *Salvia officinalis* 'Tricolor', with *Teucrium pyrenaicum* in the corner
Right: *Thymus × citriodorus* 'Silver Queen', a variegated form of the lemon thyme

grey-green. 'Tricolor' is white, pink and purple. These do not go well together, although it would be convenient if they did because they both grow to 2 ft (60 cm) and need full sun, a well-drained soil and a trim over in spring.

There are not very many variegated rock plants to choose from but *Thymus × citriodorus* 'Silver Queen' is a good one. The grey-green and silver leaves go well with the pale lilac flowers. This ground-hugging sub-shrub needs a sunny well-drained place to thrive and a trim over after flowering. If any branches revert to green, they should be cut out.

The creeping *Vinca major* 'Variegata' is not so rampageous as *Vinca minor*, but it nevertheless must be watched. It makes rotten groundcover because it has long trailing stems which root at the ends, but it is an agreeable plant to allow to wander about in an unappealing spot in dry semi-shade. The glossy oval leaves are grey-green with creamy yellow variegations. There are blue-mauve, star-shaped, periwinkle flowers in April and May and sometimes also in late summer.

DECIDUOUS SHRUBS

Actinidia kolomikta is a glorious and unusual climber. Related to the Chinese gooseberry, it has heart-shaped leaves, up to 6 in.

(15 cm) long, which begin purplish green but, as the season wears on, develop variegations — white on the pointed end of the leaves and pink nearer the centre. Sometimes the whole leaf colours, particularly if the climber is in a warm sunny spot. It is not always an easy plant to keep alive, especially in the north. It is never very vigorous and needs good support for the twining stems. (See p.56.)

Berberis thunbergii 'Rose Glow' is a very popular shrub and rightly so, although it can be difficult to place it happily. This is particularly true in spring when the leaves are splashed with different shades of pink as well as purple. Later in the season, the leaves are simply purple. (See p.56.) 'Harlequin' is quite similar, but has white speckles. These are slower-growing than the ordinary *B. thunbergii* and they will reach 4 ft (1.2 m) in a few years.

Cornus alba 'Spaethii' and 'Elegantissima' are variegated forms of the red-stemmed dogwood. The first has golden-variegated leaves, the second white mottlings and margins. They both grow up to about 8 ft (2.5 m) and, though it is tempting to try them together, they do not look especially good side by side. Being dogwoods, they like a moisture-retentive soil in sun or partial shade. They should be hard pruned in spring for maximum decorative effect.

Fuchsia magellanica 'Versicolor' lives up to its name and is graceful but not very vigorous. The leaves are a satisfactory mixture of colours – grey-green, pink and creamy white, particularly on the young shoots. The form *gracilis* 'Variegata' has creamy yellow margins, but is less strong in constitution even than 'Versicolor'. Both have slender red and purple flowers and grow best in a sheltered sunny place. These shrubs are usually cut down by frost in winter but, once established, are unlikely to be killed by it. They are choice enough to deserve protection anyway.

Hypericum × moserianum 'Tricolor' has very interesting variegation, namely, grey-green leaves with reddish pink and white markings. This is not especially enhanced by the long-lasting yellow flowers. It is a small, open, even a little scruffy, shrub, which sends up arching stems to about 2 ft (60 cm) and flowers from July until October. It may die back in winter and new growth will not emerge until May.

Parthenocissus henryana is a self-clinging relation of the Virginia creeper, with dark green, five-lobed leaves which have silvery pink veins. It is a very vigorous climber, but requires some shelter, relishing a west or north west wall. The variegation becomes more pronounced as autumn approaches and the leaves turn bright red before falling. No one notices the flowers at midsummer.

Symphoricarpos orbiculatus 'Foliis Variegatus' is a great improvement on the very dull, green snowberry. It is a dense shrub with

Above (left): *Actinidia kolomikta* should be grown on a sunny wall for the most pronounced variegation; (right) the silvery markings of *Parthenocissus henryana* are more strongly defined in partial shade
Below: *Berberis thunbergii* 'Rose Glow' is a charming small shrub which was introduced in 1965

Left: A remarkable mixture of colours in the foliage of *Ajuga reptans* 'Multicolor'
Right: *Pleioblastus auricomus* is a beautiful sight in full leaf in late summer

leaves which are round and irregularly margined with yellow. Do not plant it in too shady a place or the variegation will be less obvious and may disappear. The flowers are pale pink and the berries purplish red.

PERENNIALS

Ajuga reptans 'Multicolor' has received a mention in the introduction to this chapter for the amount of colours to be discerned on the leaf. The flowers are the typical blue-mauve bugle flowers in April and May. There is another form called 'Variegata' which has creamy white margins to the grey-green leaves. Both make good groundcover in rich soil and semi-shade.

Carex oshimensis 'Evergold' is a sedge with evergreen arching leaves up to 8 in. (20 cm) long; these are golden yellow with thin green margins. It always looks neat whatever the time of year and very much appreciates a moist position.

Fragaria vesca 'Variegata' is the variegated wild strawberry. It has a fresh bright look about it because of the uneven splashes of creamy white on a dark green background. It likes to grow in part-shade and will meander about agreeably without becoming a menace.

Glyceria maxima 'Variegata' thrives in heavy moist soil, for it is really a waterside grass, and it can become unmanageable if the

Left: *Hosta sieboldiana* 'Frances Williams', originally known as 'Gold Edge'
Right: *Iris pallida* 'Variegata' has very effective white-striped leaves

conditions suit. However, it will survive quite well in dryish soil. The leaves are pinkish in spring, then striped green, yellow and white when mature, on stems up to 4 ft (1.2 m).

There are so many good variegated hostas that a favourite is hard to choose, but I do think *Hosta sieboldiana* 'Frances Williams' is exceptional. The leaves are dark blue-green and corrugated, with thick yellow margins. It really is a good colour combination. There are other worthy ones, like *Hosta ventricosa* 'Aureomarginata', which has yellow- or cream-margined foliage with blue flowers in late summer; and the similar *Hosta crispula* with white-edged leaves.

Iris pallida 'Variegata' is just one of several good white- or yellow-striped irises. It has pretty blue-mauve flowers in June. It needs a reasonably sunny well-drained place to thrive. *Iris pseudacorus* 'Variegata', on the other hand, which has yellow-striped leaves, flourishes in bogs or shallow water. It produces yellow flowers in June, after which the variegation on the leaves fades.

Miscanthus sinensis 'Variegatus' and 'Zebrinus' are two forms of a very useful, tall, ornamental grass. The first grows to about 5 ft (1.5 m), the second a little more, but neither is invasive. 'Zebrinus', the zebra grass, has yellow bands on the green leaves after mid-summer, whereas 'Variegatus' has white stripes. They have feathery flower heads in October. They do best in moist soil, in sun or part-shade.

Above: The striking *Symphytum* × *uplandicum* 'Variegatum' appreciates some shade
Below: *Silybum marianum* will grow in any ordinary soil

Molinia caerulea var. *caerulea* 'Variegata' is a grass with neat foliage, up to 1½ ft (45 cm) high, and feathery flower stems, up to 3 ft (1 m), in autumn. The leaves are thin, first erect and then arching, and green striped with cream. This is another plant for a moist soil in sun or semi-shade.

Persicaria virginiana 'Painter's Palette' has branching stems of oval leaves, splashed with pink, grey and cream. There is a distinctive deep red "V" in the middle of each leaf. The flowers are insignificant. It likes a rich soil in semi-shade.

Phormium cookianum ssp. *hookeri* 'Cream Delight' is one of the best of these not very hardy New Zealand flaxes. Generally speaking, phormiums are not plants for cold places but, if you have a sheltered warm position in a moisture-retentive soil, this one grows to about 3 ft (1 m) and has a cream band in the centre of the ascending leaves, which bend over towards the top. It is smaller than *Phormium tenax* and, to my mind, less bizarre as an accent plant.

Pleioblastus auricomus is a bamboo which grows to about 4 ft (1.2 m). The leaves are green with yellow stripes; the variegation is brightest in full sun. This is one of the better-behaved bamboos because it is clump-forming and therefore not invasive.

Sedum telephium 'Variegatum' is a curious rather than strictly pretty version of the ice plant. The leaves are blue-green with creamy yellow variegations; the flowers in late summer are pink. All-green shoots are apt to appear and have to be cut out. It grows to about 1¼ ft (40 cm) tall and looks best in a group.

Symphytum × *uplandicum* 'Variegatum' is very robust and well-variegated all summer. This plant looks best when the mauve and pink flowers are not out. It makes a basal rosette up to 3 ft (1 m) of large, sage-green, grey- and cream-margined, oval, hairy leaves. (See p.59.)

BIENNIALS

Silybum marianum is a very exciting plant, even if it is meat and drink to aphids. It is known as Our Lady's milk thistle and, if you let it, has tall heads of mauve thistle flowers. The oval lobed leaves in a basal rosette are a dark shiny green, heavily marbled with white veins. This is a biennial but, unfortunately, it is not available from all seedsmen. However, it is worth seeking out. (See p.59.)

Acer palmatum 'Dissectum Atropurpureum' in autumn

List of Nurseries

Mail order nurseries which have good supplies of foliage plants:
Bressingham Gardens, Diss, Norfolk IP22 2AB
Great Dixter Nurseries, Northiam, Rye, East Sussex TN31 6PH
Hillier Nurseries (Winchester) Ltd, Ampfield House, Ampfield, Romsey, Hampshire, SO5 9PA
Holden Clough Nursery, Holden, Bolton-by-Bowland, Clitheroe, Lancashire BB7 4PF
Hopleys Plants, Much Hadham, Hertfordshire SG10 6BU
Notcutts Nurseries, Woodbridge, Suffolk IP12 4AF
Unusual Plants, White Barn House, Elmstead Market, Colchester, Essex CO7 7DP

For seeds:
Chiltern Seeds, Bortree Stile, Ulverston, Cumbria LA12 7PB
Thompson & Morgan, London Road, Ipswich, Suffolk IP2 0BA

Index of plants